LET'S BEGAIN

LET'S BE OPTIMSTIC AND
DO OUR BEST

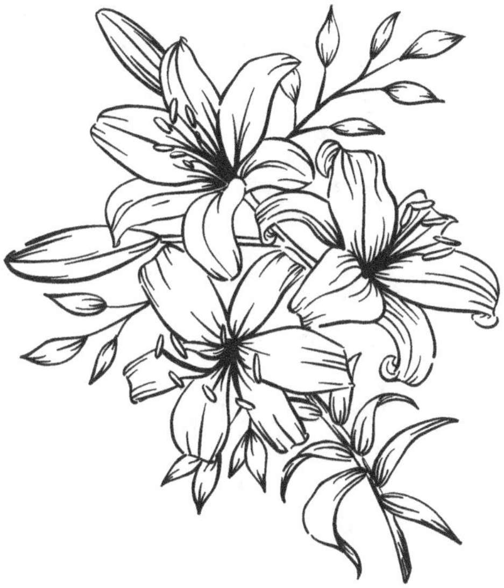

BELONGS TO

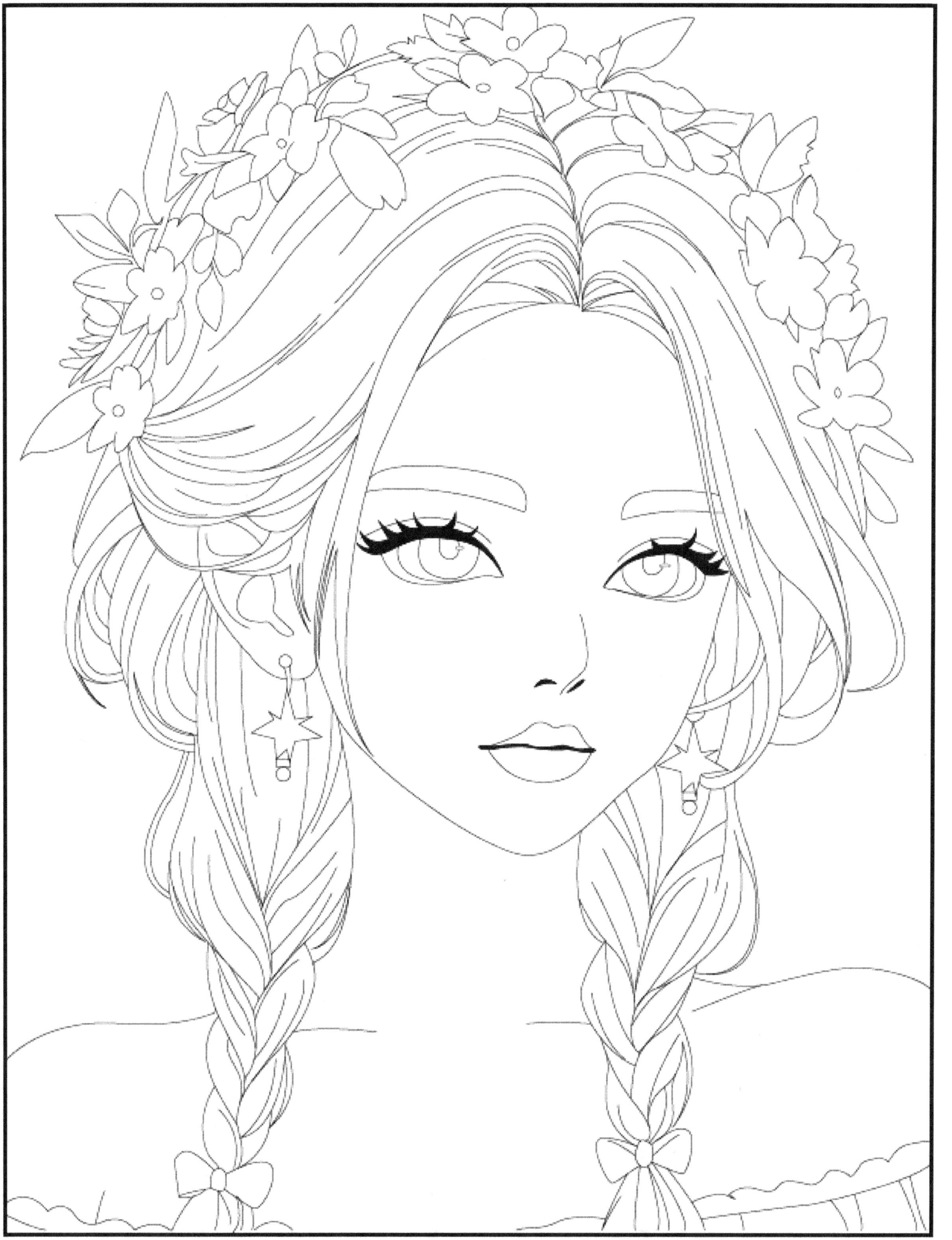

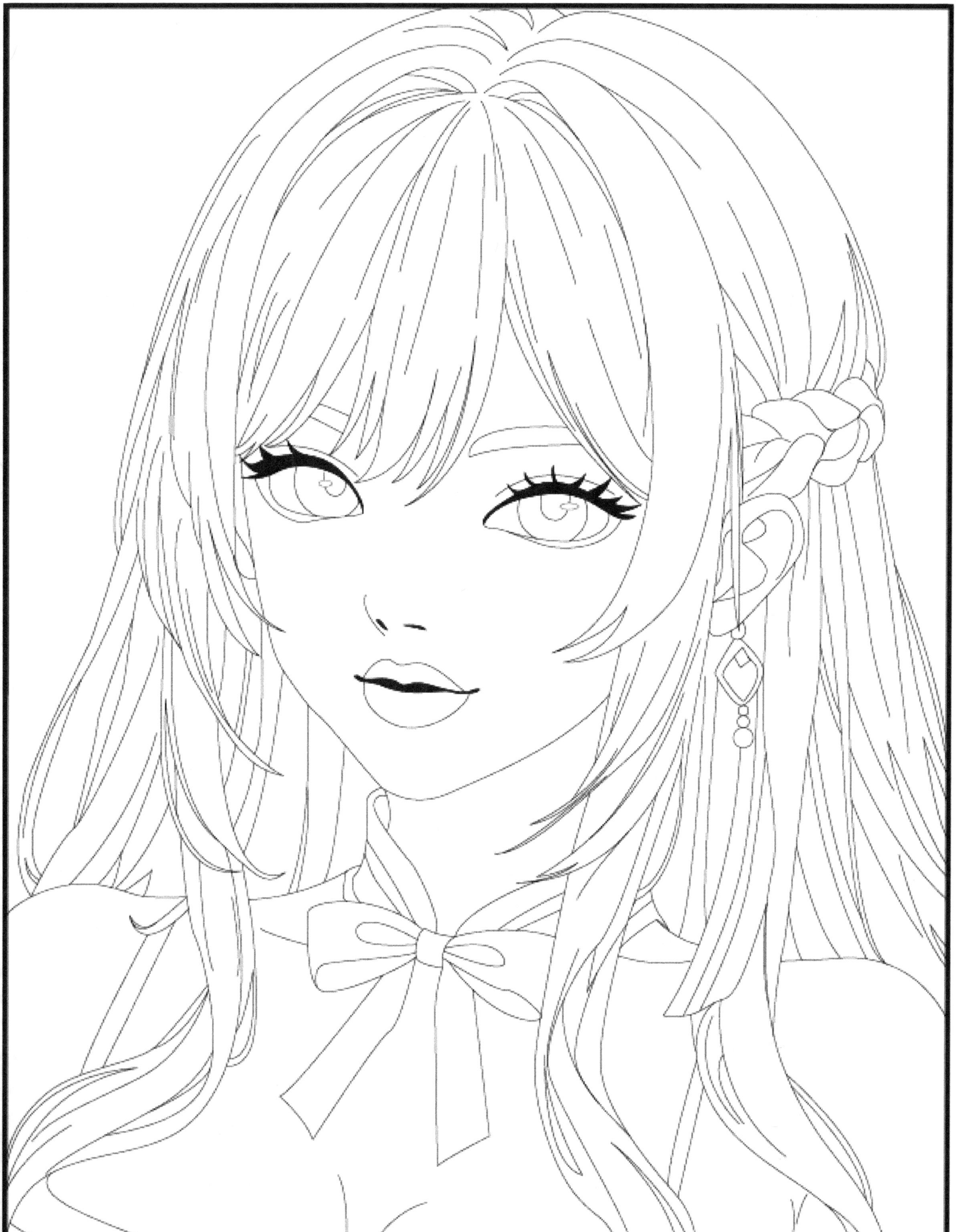

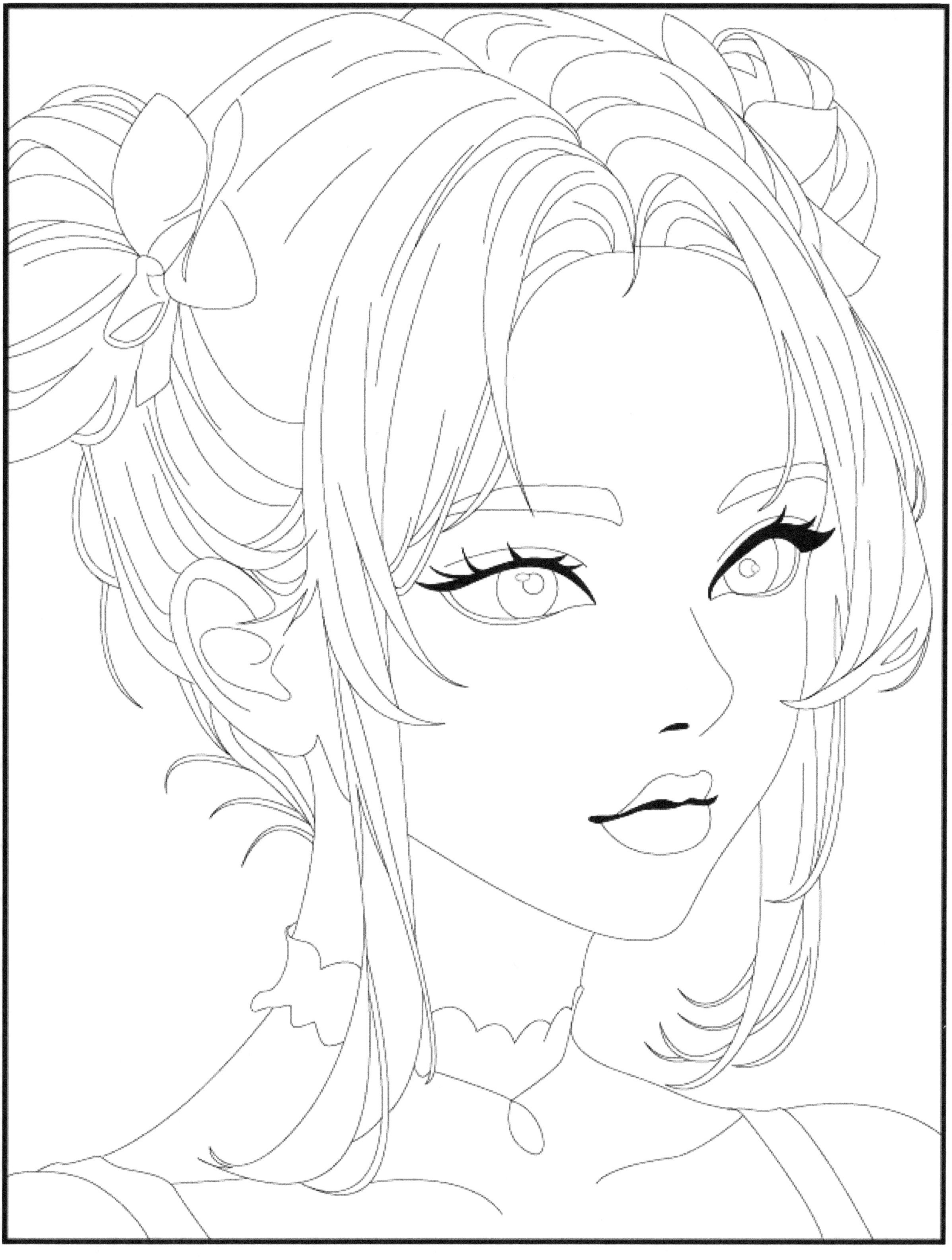

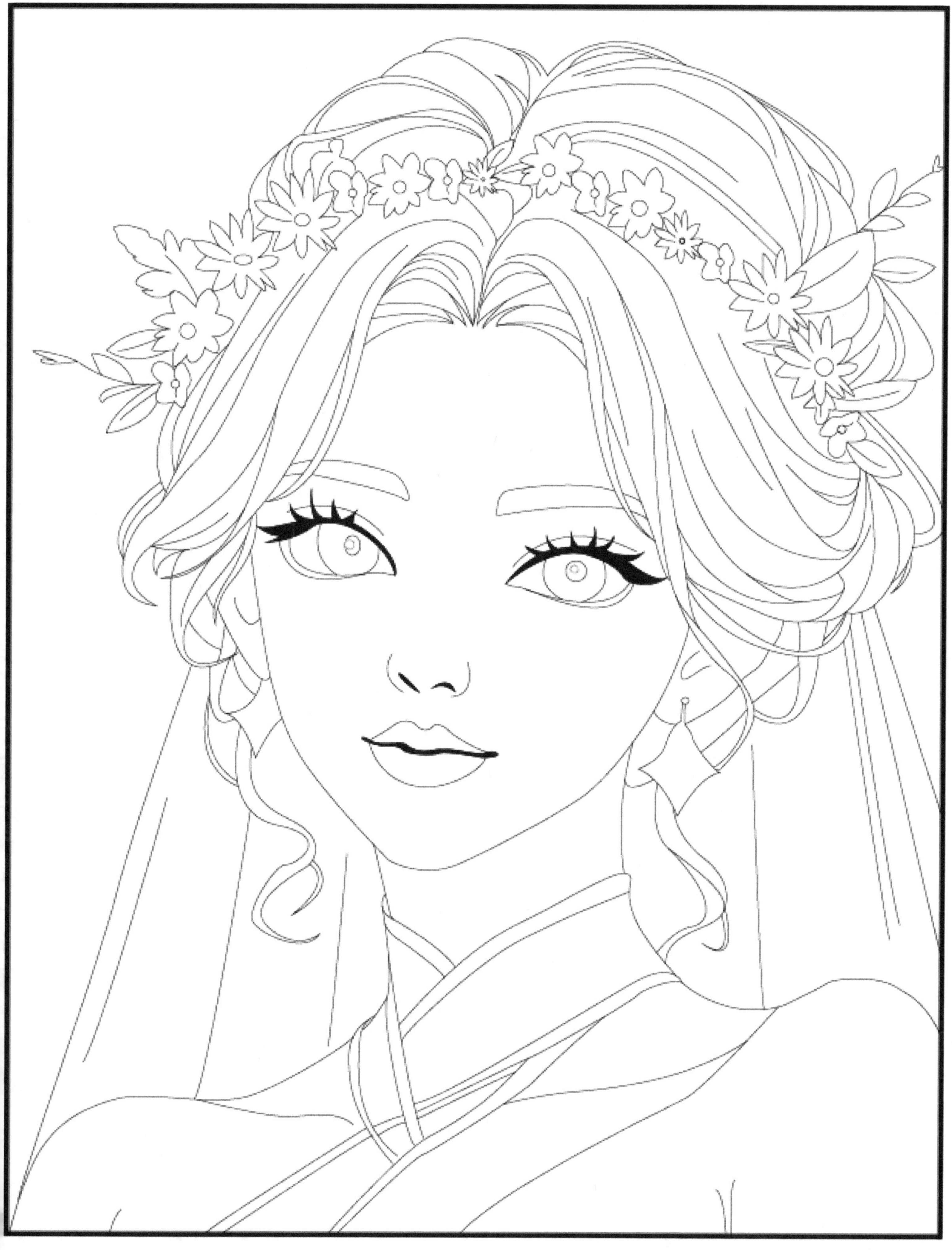

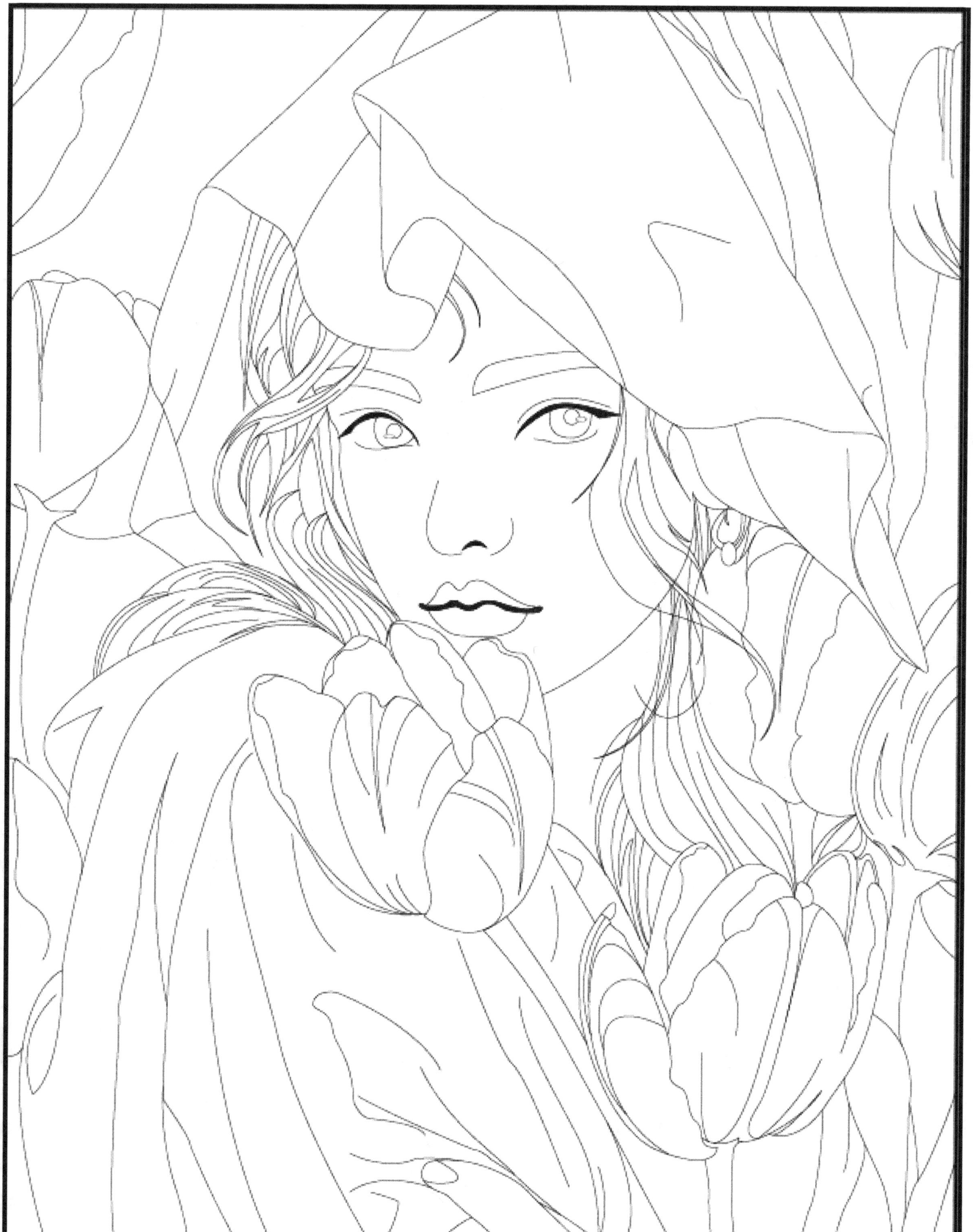

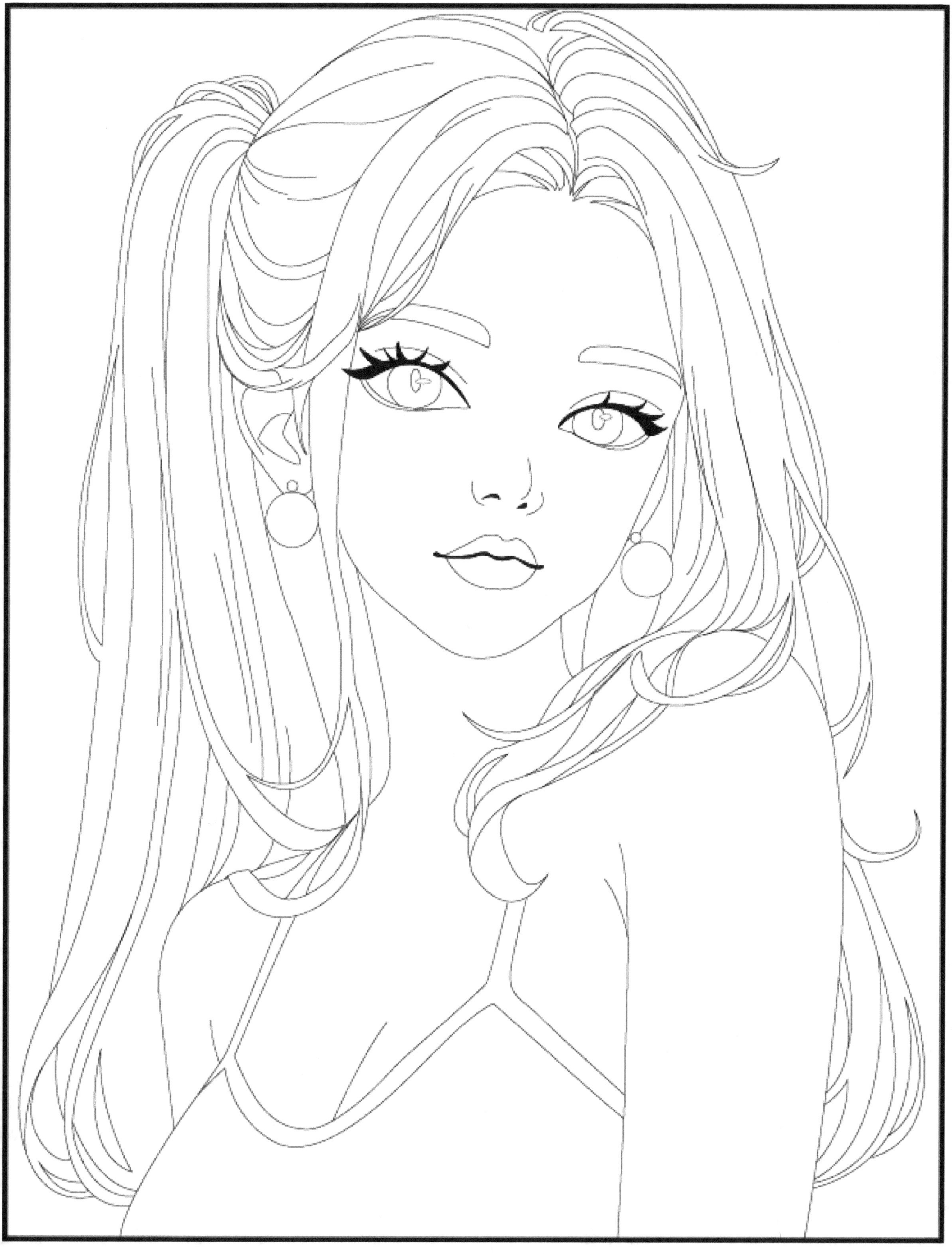

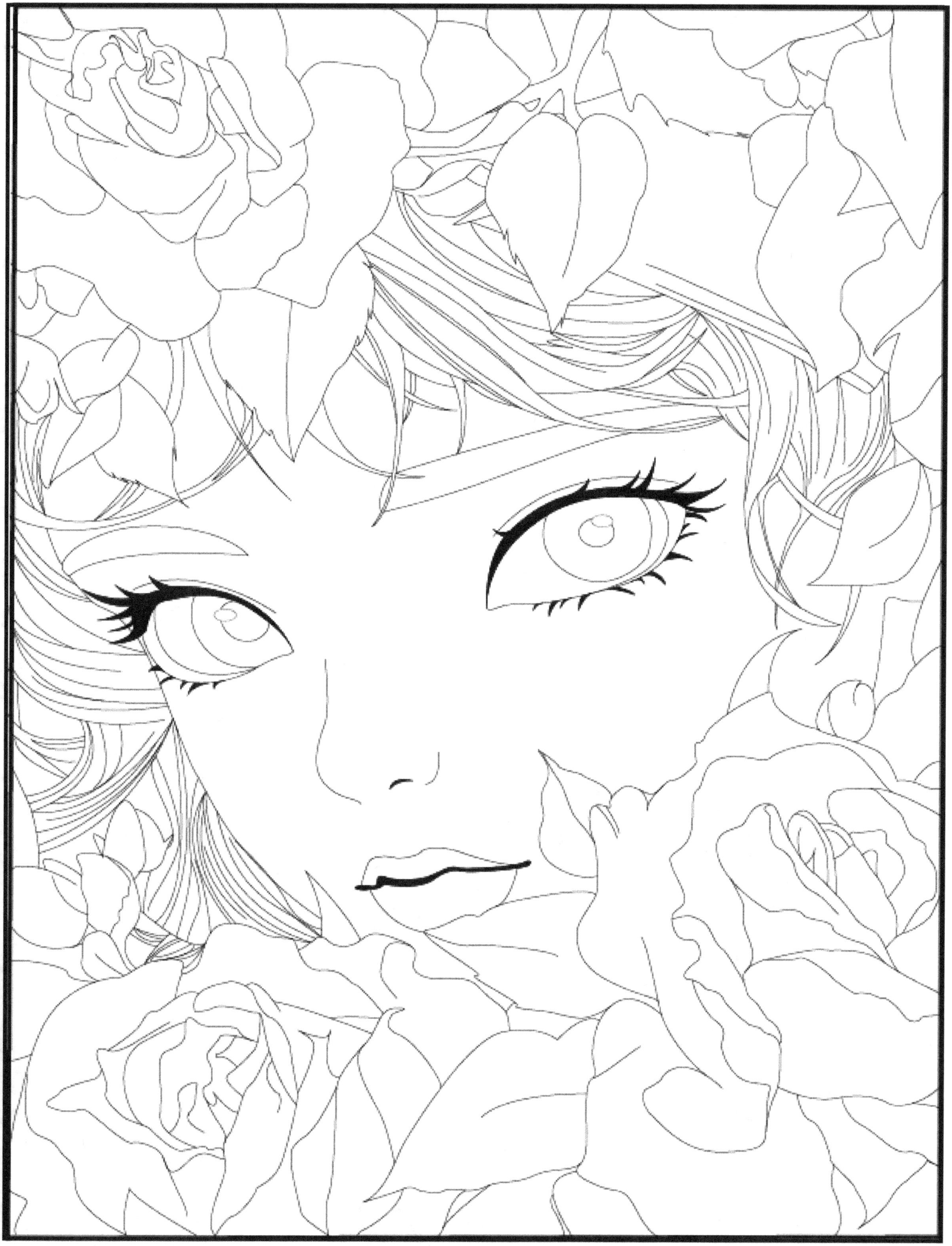

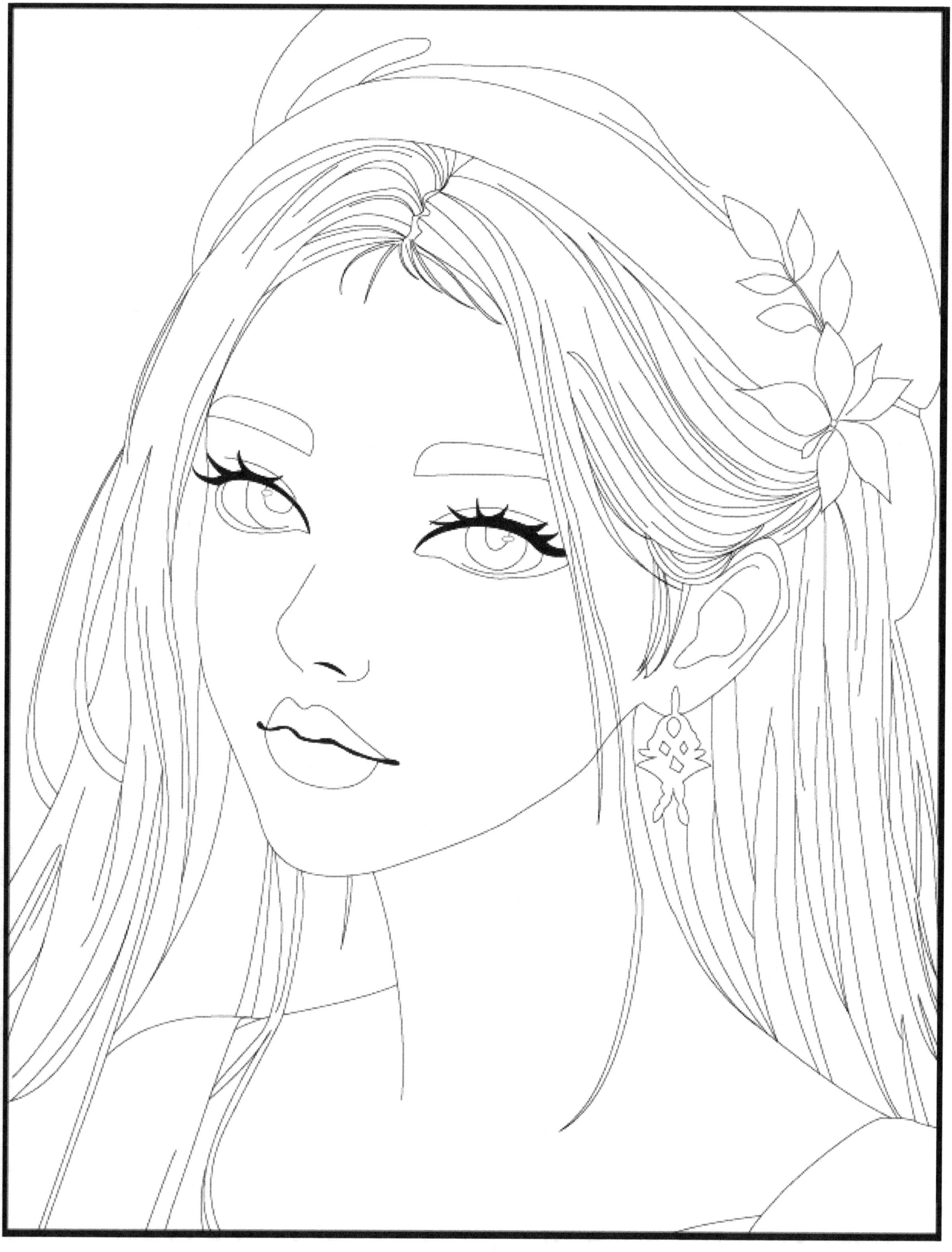

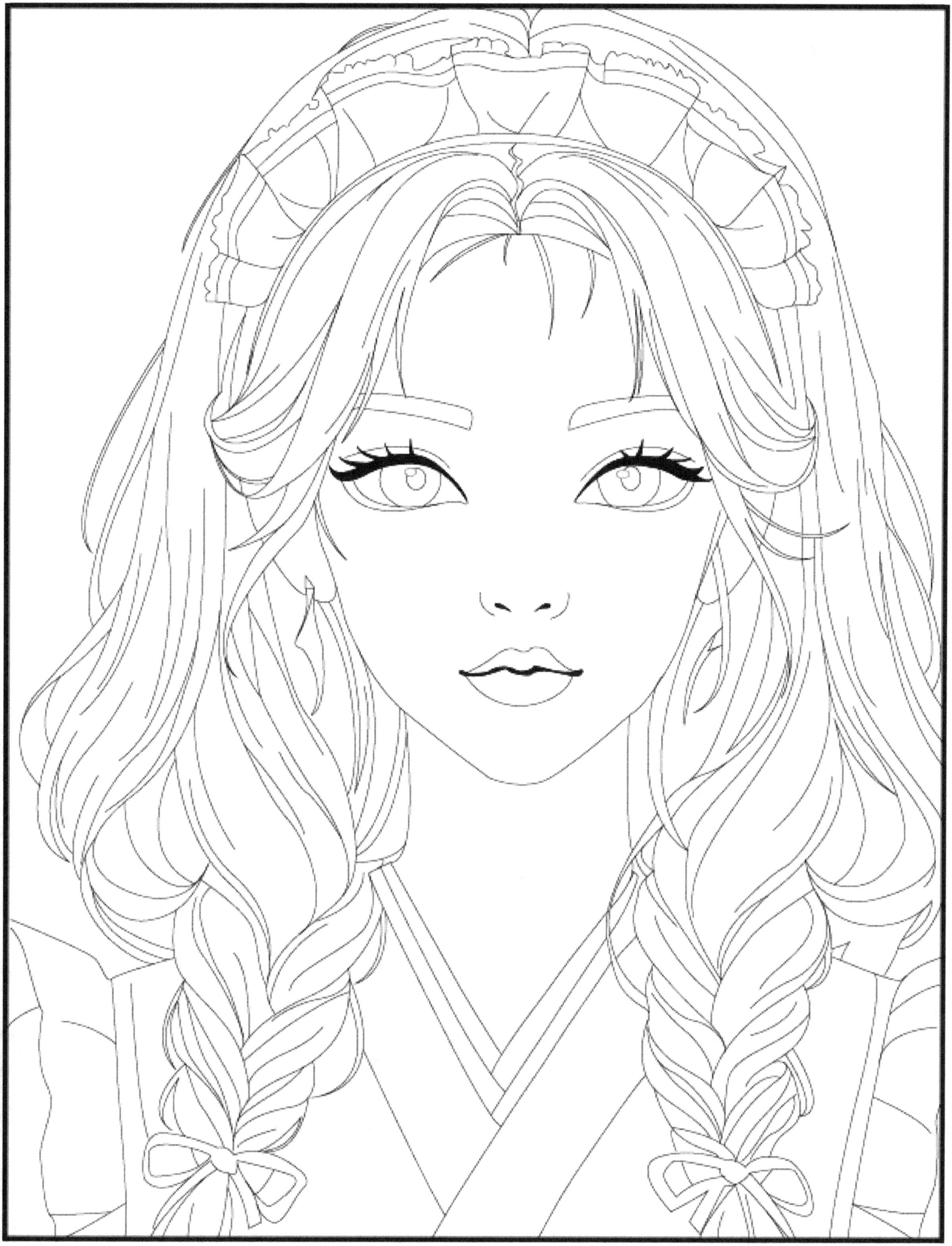

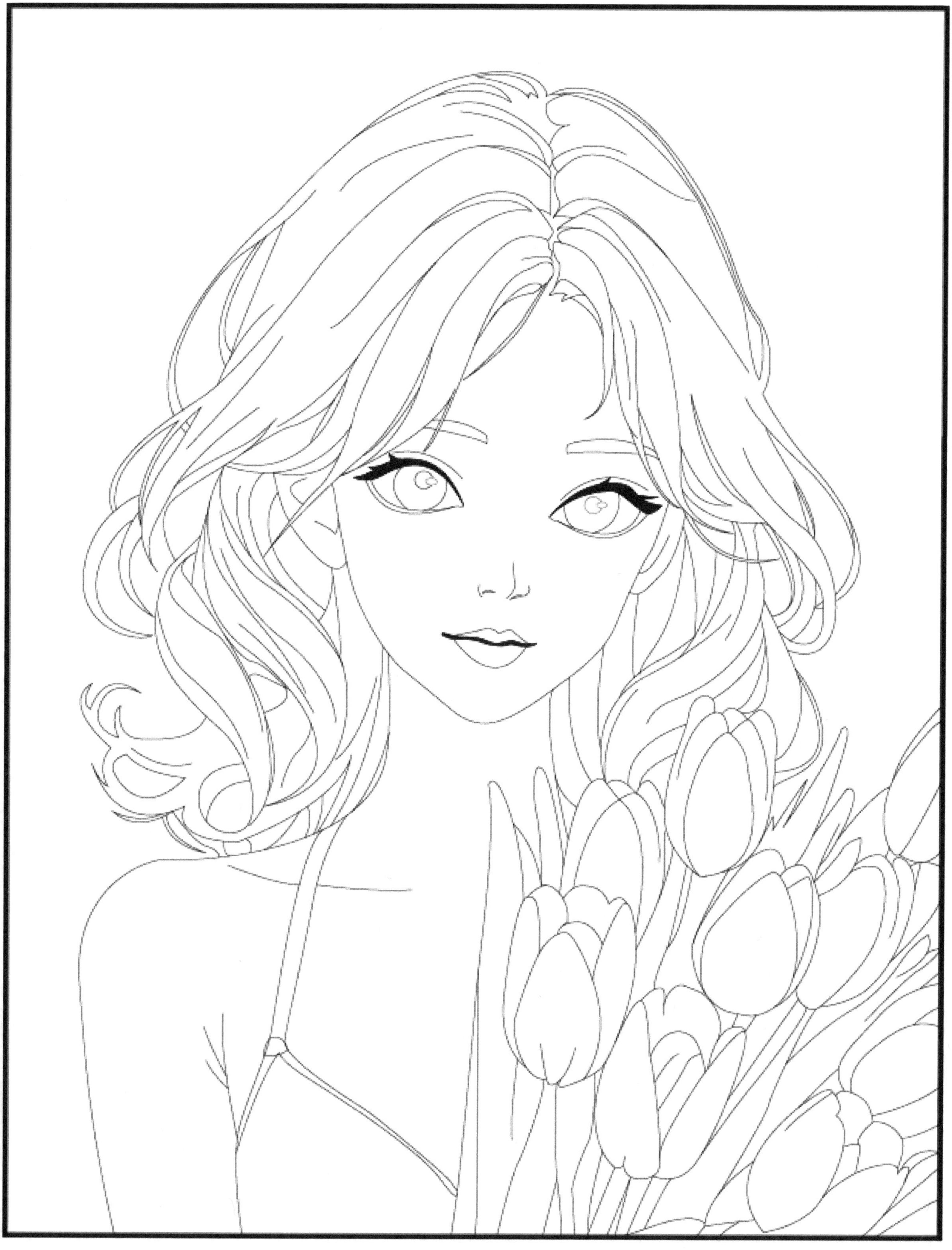

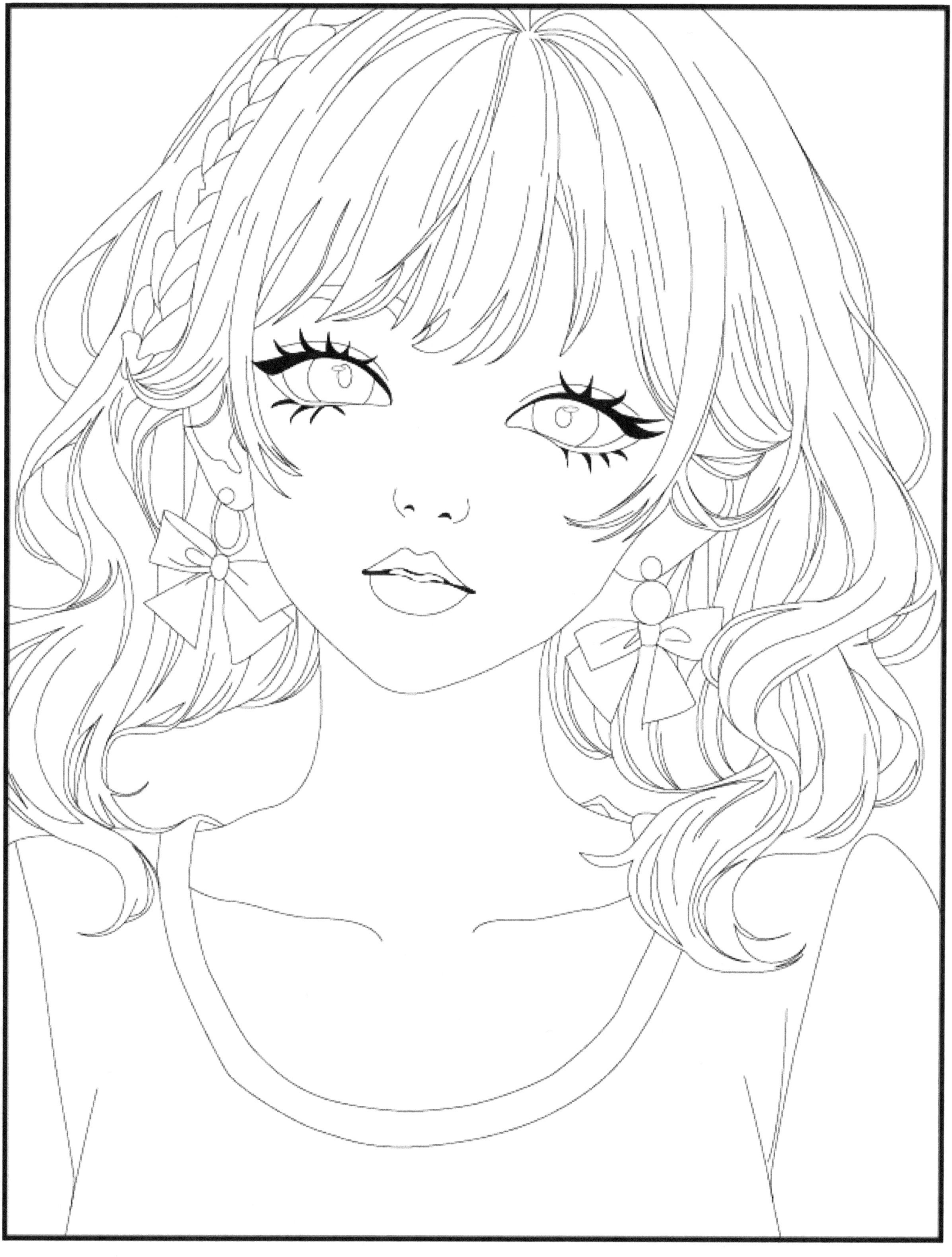

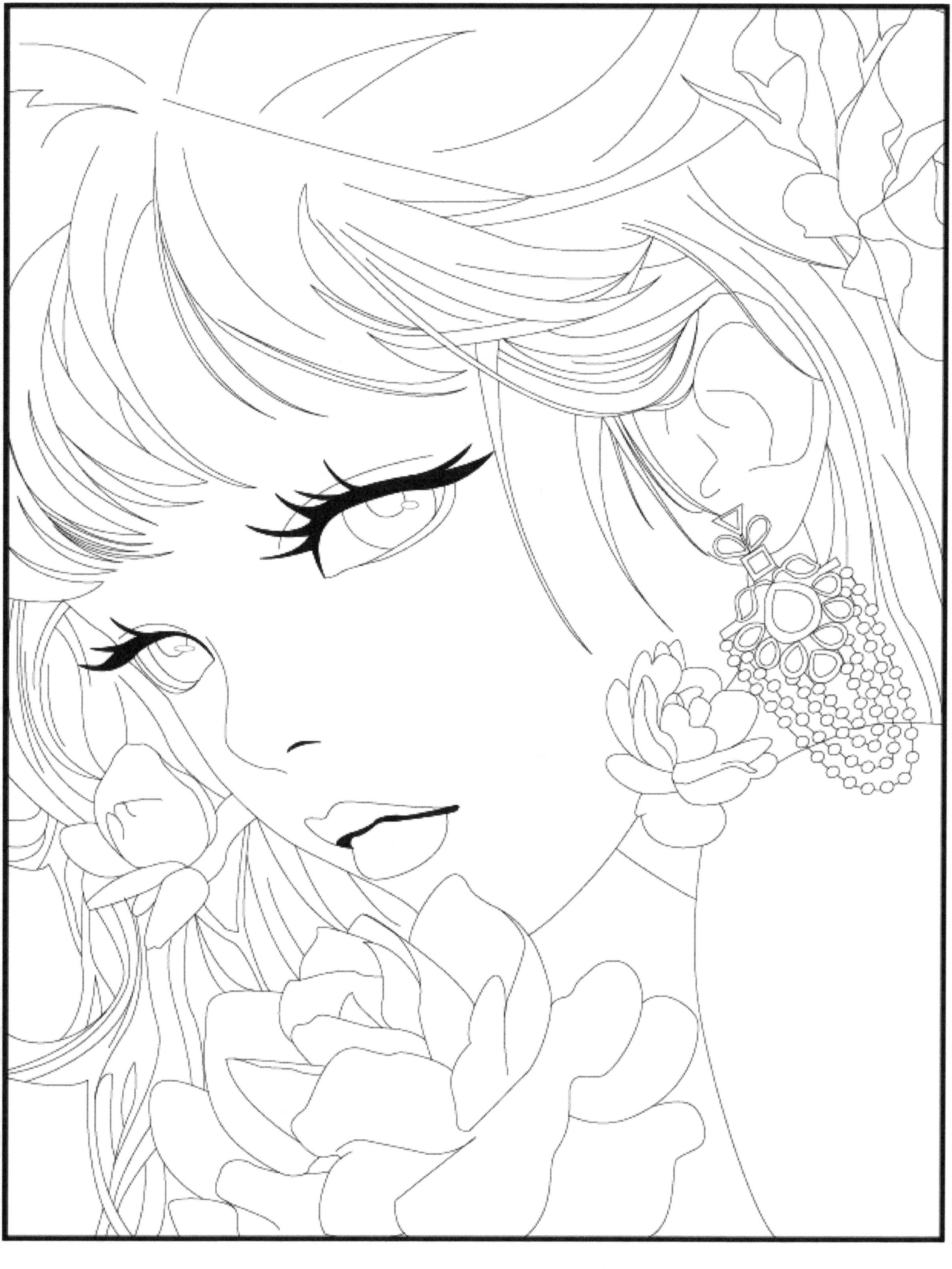

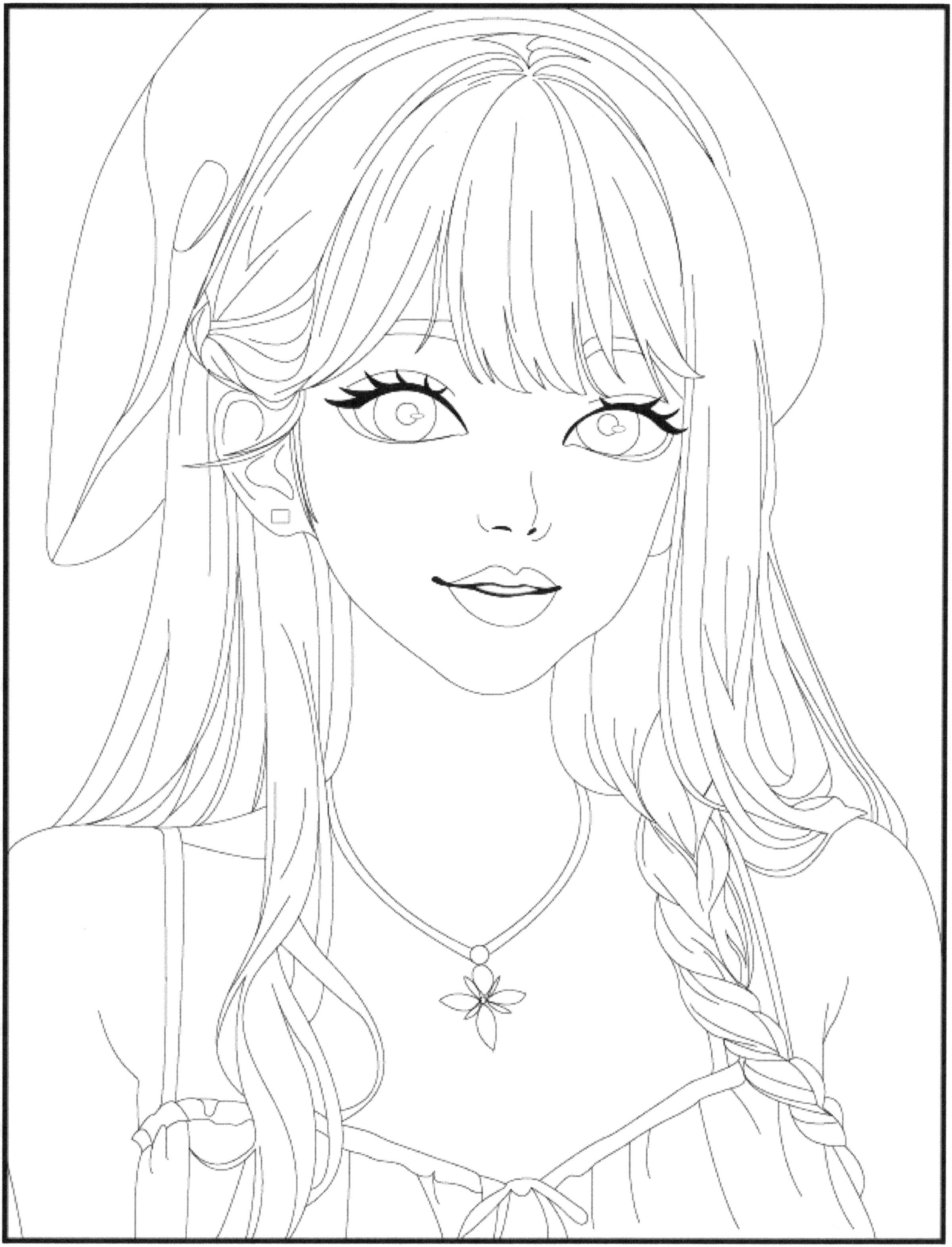

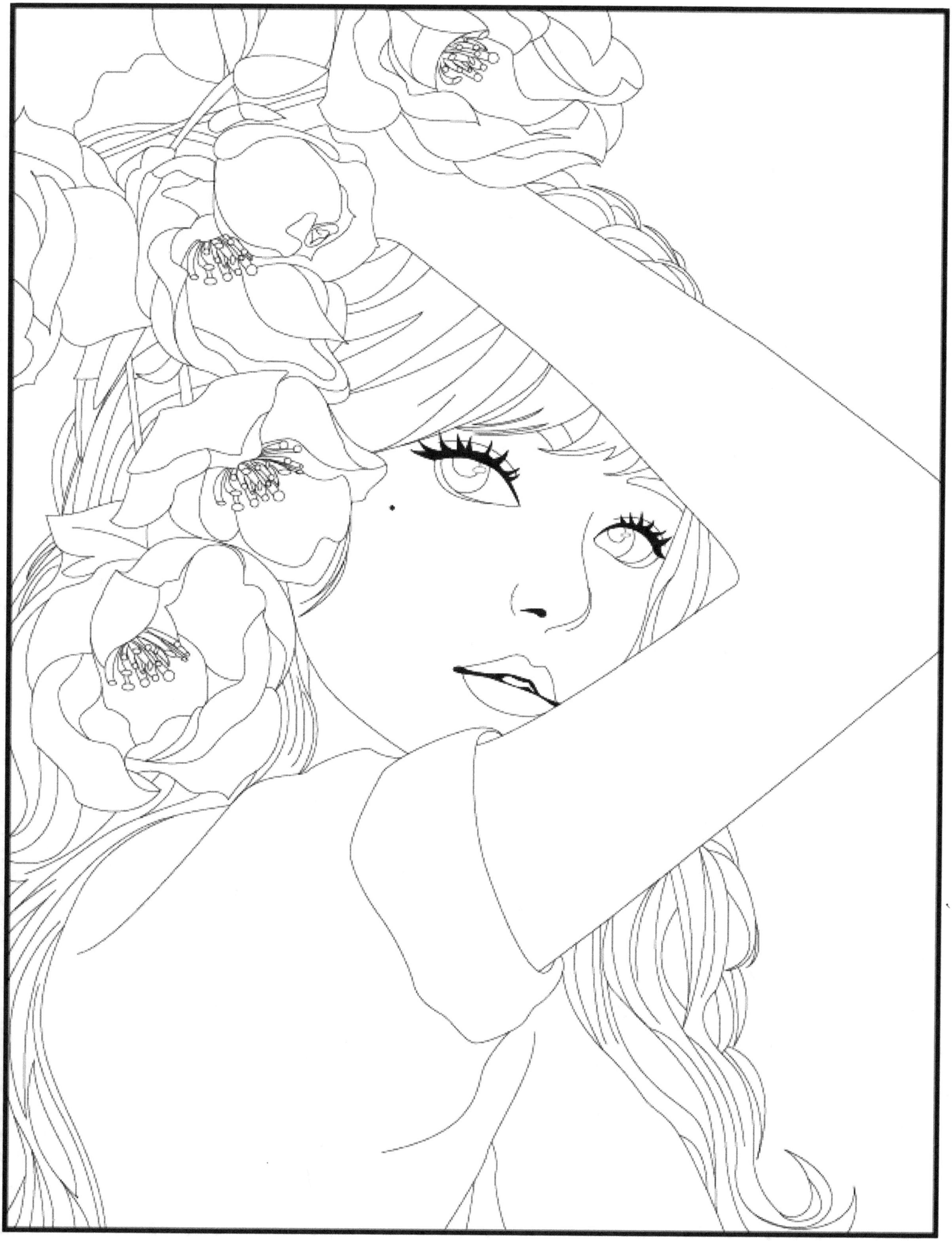

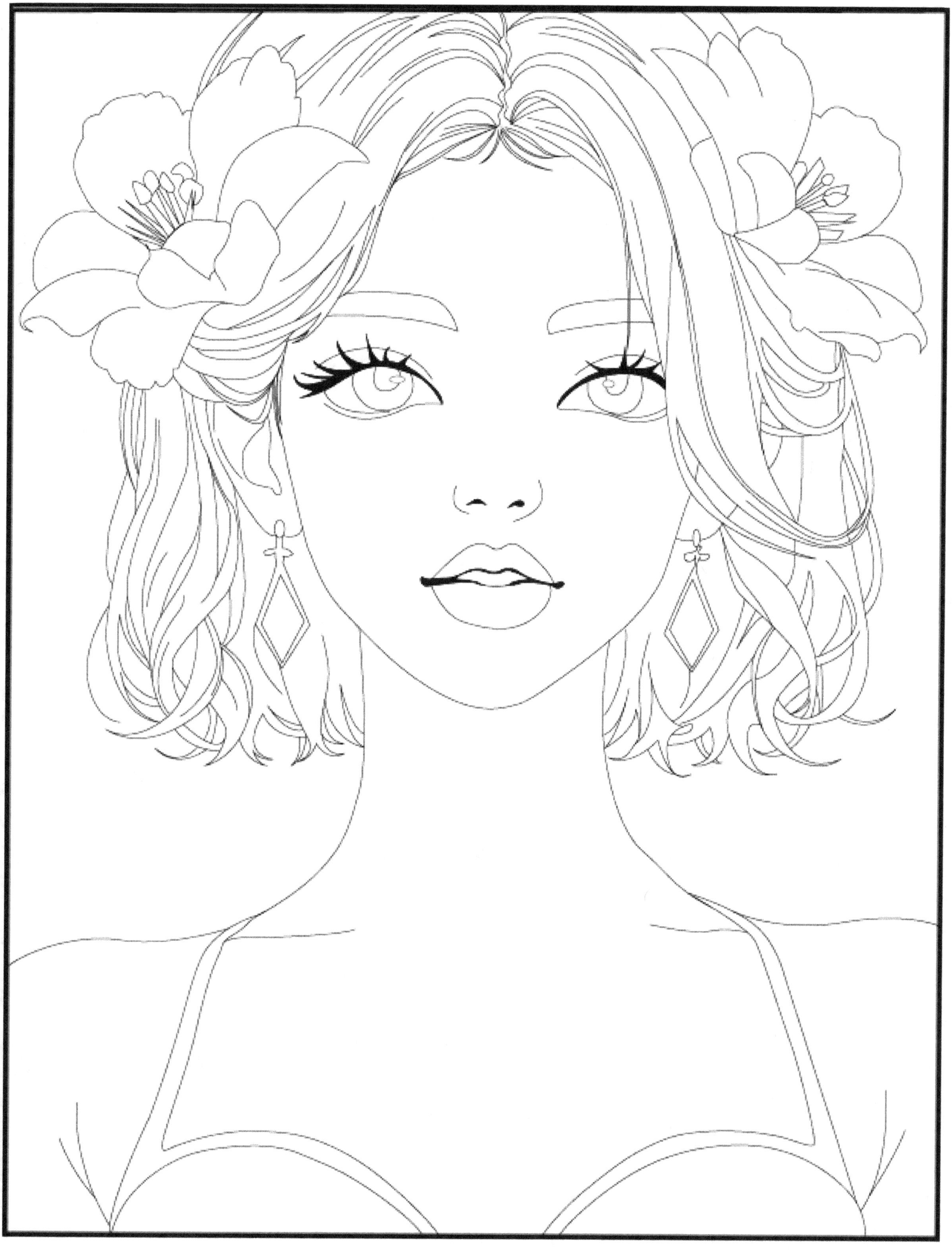

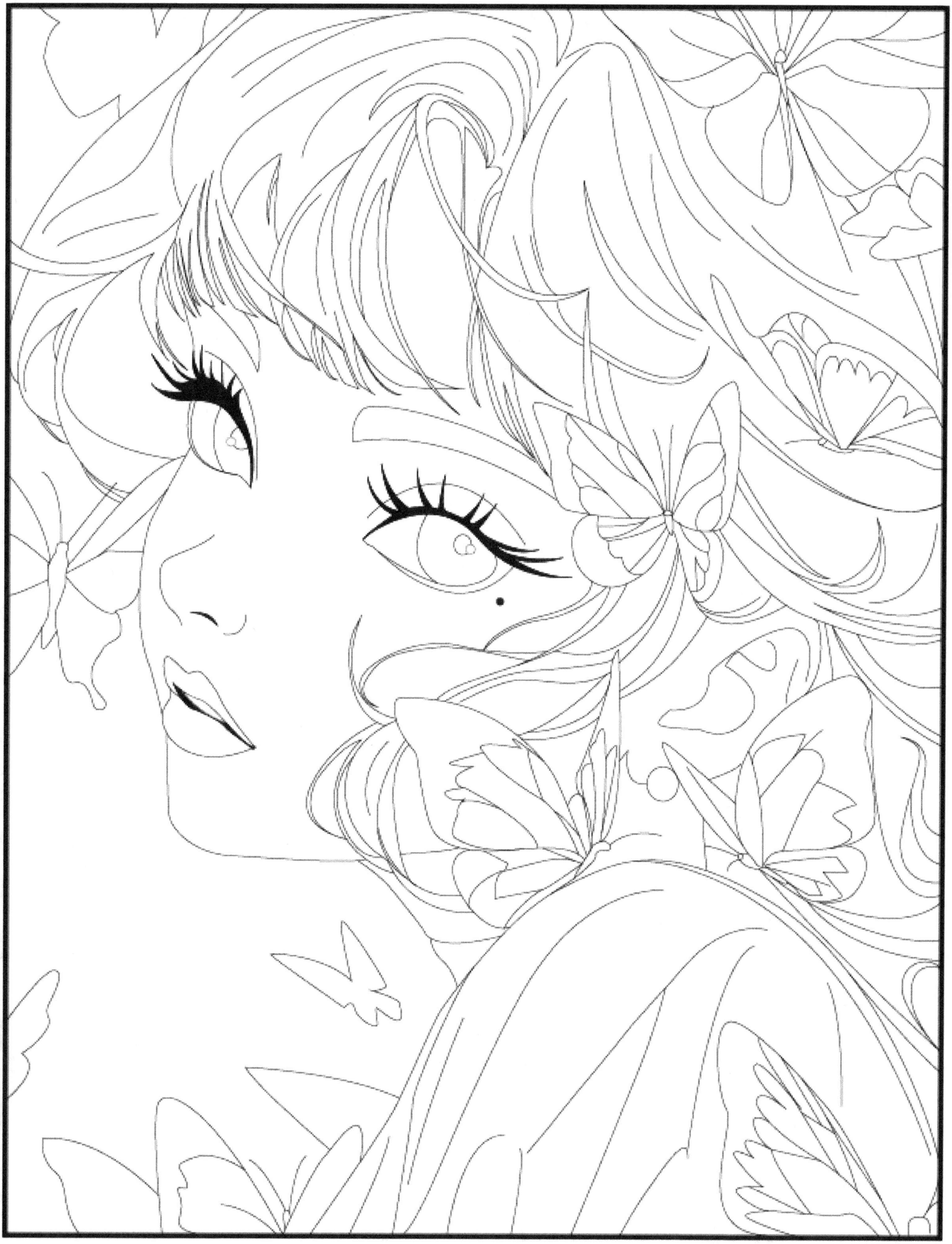

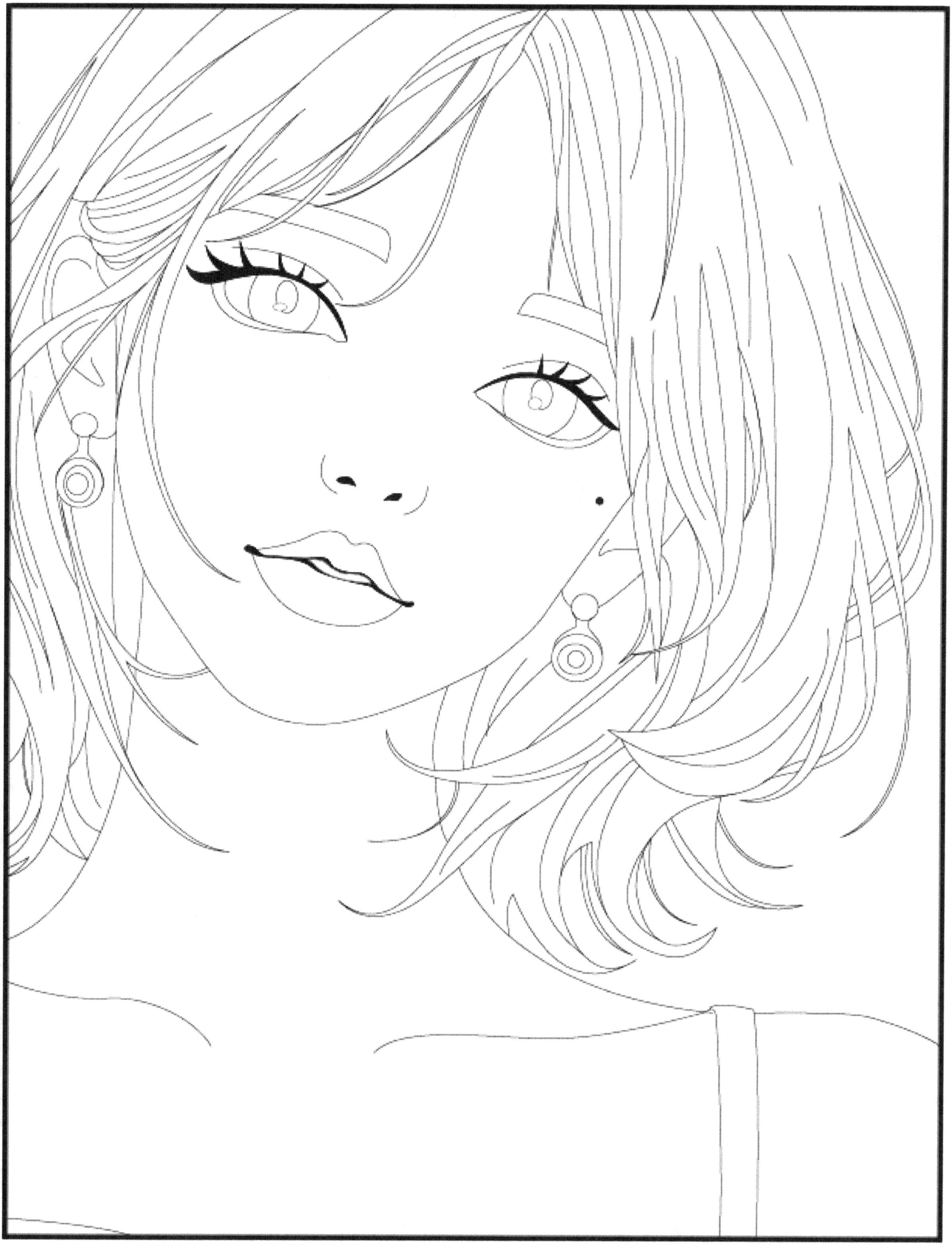

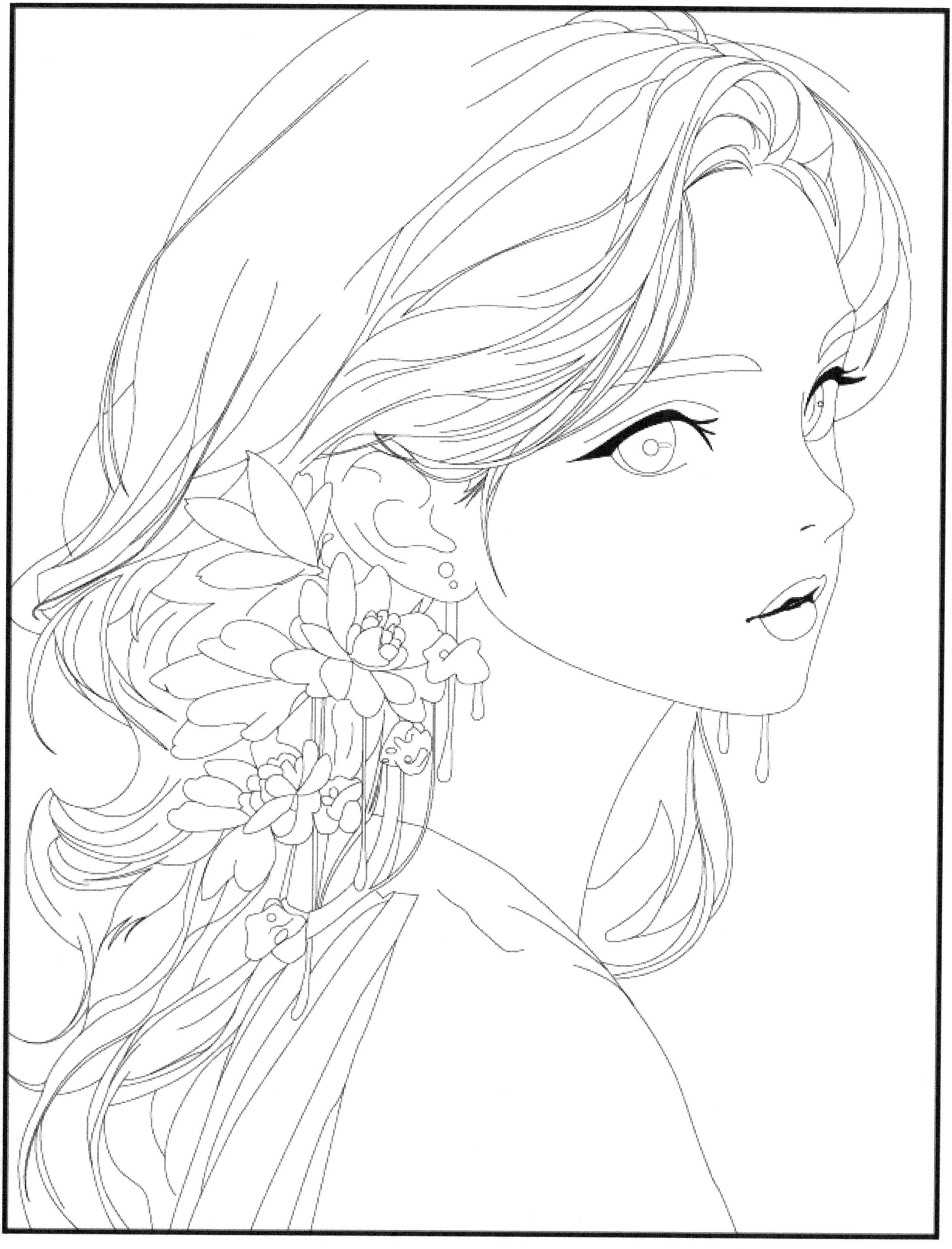

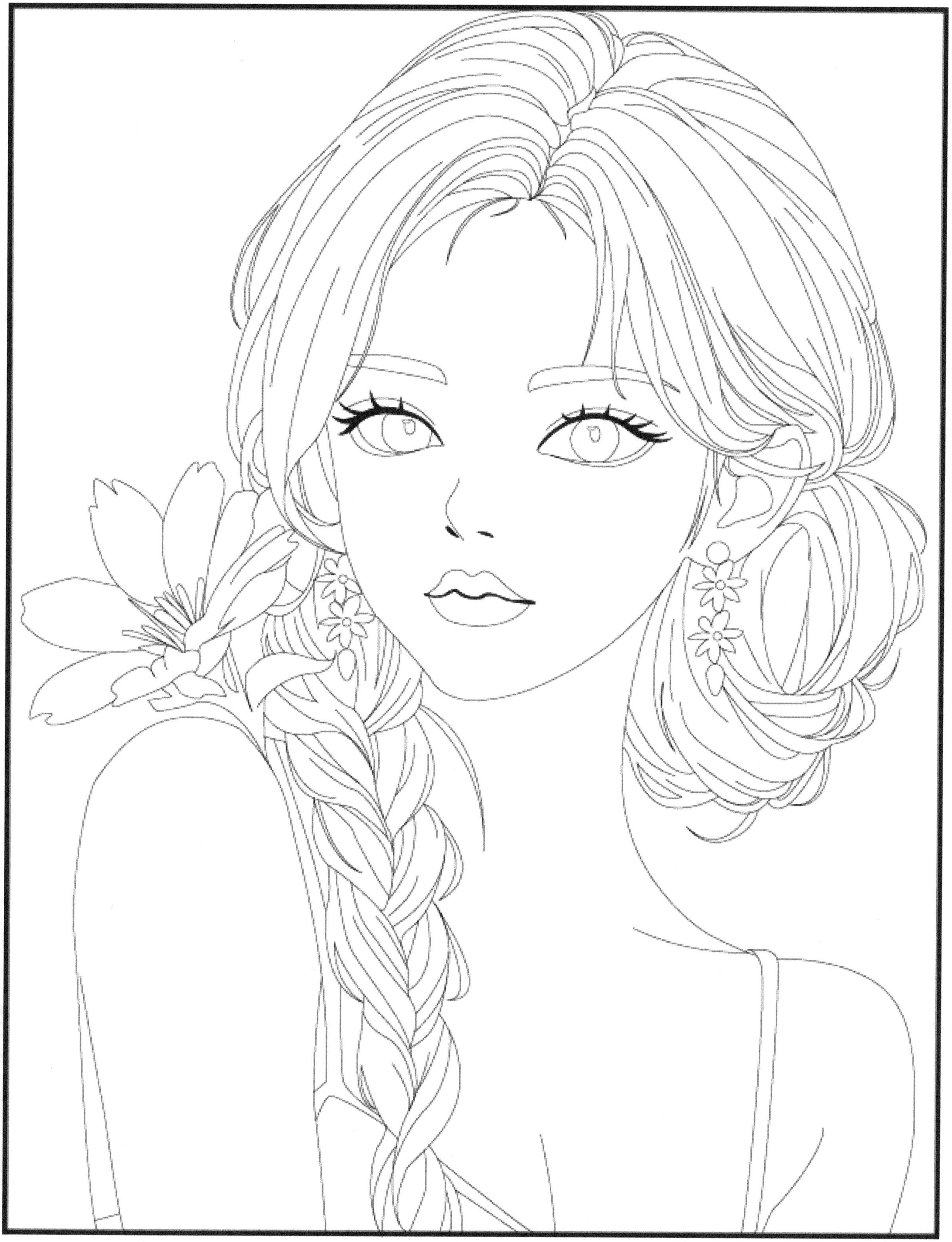

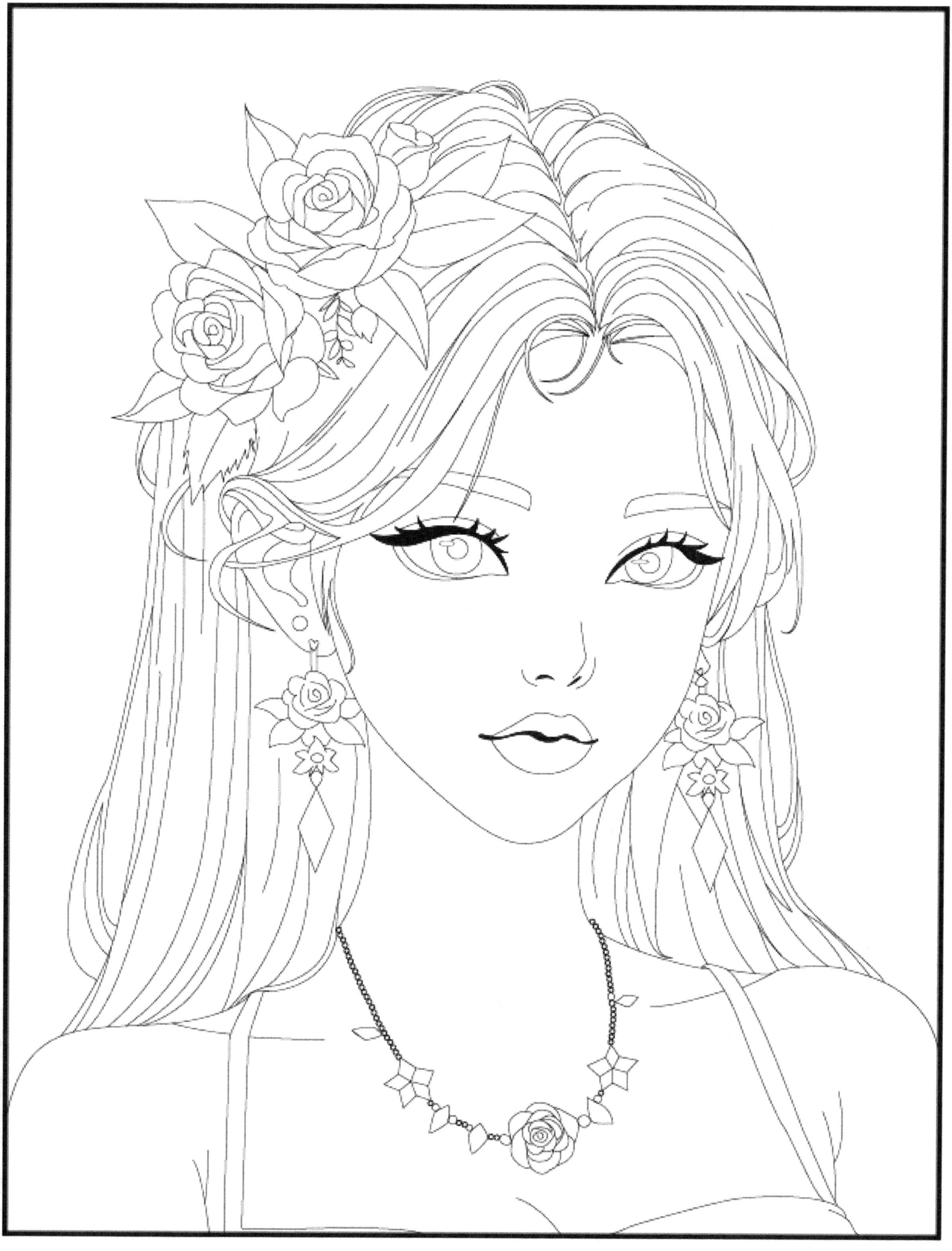

www.ingramcontent.com/pod-product-compliance
Lightning Source LLC
Chambersburg PA
CBHW081020240526
45471CB00018B/3911
* 9 7 9 8 3 2 1 2 1 9 7 4 4 *